WHEN DID
IGNORANCE
BECOME A POINT OF VIEW?

Other DILBERT books from Andrews McMeel Publishing

Excuse Me While I Wag
ISBN: 0-7407-1390-6

Dilbert-A Treasury of Sunday Strips: Version 00
ISBN: 0-7407-0531-8

Random Acts of Management
ISBN: 0-7407-0453-2

Dilbert Gives You the Business
ISBN: 0-7407-0338-2 hardcover
ISBN: 0-7407-0003-0 paperback

Don't Step in the Leadership
ISBN: 0-8362-7844-5

Journey to Cubeville
ISBN: 0-8362-7175-0 hardcover
ISBN: 0-8362-6745-1 paperback

I'm Not Anti-Business, I'm Anti-Idiot
ISBN: 0-8362-5182-2

Seven Years of Highly Defective People
ISBN: 0-8362-5129-6 hardcover
ISBN: 0-8362-3668-8 paperback

Casual Day Has Gone Too Far
ISBN: 0-8362-2899-5

Fugitive from the Cubicle Police
ISBN: 0-8362-2119-2

Still Pumped from Using the Mouse
ISBN: 0-8362-1026-3

It's Obvious You Won't Survive by Your Wits Alone
ISBN: 0-8362-0415-8

Bring Me the Head of Willy the Mailboy!
ISBN: 0-8362-1779-9

Shave the Whales
ISBN: 0-8362-1740-3

Dogbert's Clues for the Clueless
ISBN: 0-8362-1737-3

Build a Better Life by Stealing Office Supplies
ISBN: 0-8362-1757-8

Always Postpone Meetings with Time-Wasting Morons
ISBN: 0-8362-1758-6

For ordering information, call 1-800-642-6480.

WHEN DID
IGNORANCE
BECOME A POINT OF VIEW?

A DILBERT™ BOOK
BY SCOTT ADAMS

**Andrews McMeel
Publishing**

Kansas City

When Did Ignorance Become a Point of View? copyright © 2001 by United Feature Syndicate, Inc. All rights reserved. Printed in the United States of America. No part of this book may be used or reproduced in any manner whatsoever without written permission except in the case of reprints in the context of reviews. For information, write Andrews McMeel Publishing, an Andrews McMeel Universal company, 4520 Main Street, Kansas City, Missouri 64111.

01 02 03 04 05 BAH 10 9 8 7 6 5 4 3 2 1

ISBN: 0-7407-1839-8

Library of Congress Catalog Card Number: 2001087649

For Tom-a-to and Tom-ah-to's mother

Introduction

Recently a woman called me and said she had no idea who I was but she had been told by someone—she couldn't remember who—that I give money to people like her. The woman said that she and her husband had nine kids and had moved to a desert in the Middle East. Now they were having difficulty supporting themselves because, well, they had nine kids and had moved to a desert. She figured the best solution was to call me and ask if I would support the entire family indefinitely. If you have nine children and think it's a good idea to move to the desert it is fair to say that you are not a good decision maker. So the question I had to ask myself was this: If I gave her money, would she be more likely to a) use it to feed and educate her children, or b) grunt out nine more children and move to a dislodged glacier floating in the Arctic Ocean?

The interesting part of the conversation came after I politely declined her invitation to fund the nonstop production of doomed babies. She got mad at me. Apparently she analyzed her situation and came to the conclusion that the root cause of her problem was the unwillingness of total strangers in other countries to give her money. And her solution to that problem was to get angry.

You might be wondering, as I was, whether this woman was actually a con artist who wasn't very good at her job, possibly an intern or a trainee. Maybe the experienced con artists in her office were playing a practical joke on her: "Tell him you're stupid and you need money to produce more people like you." I'll never know the real story. But it reminded me of all the times that my point of view differed from other people's.

For example, our current system of world government involves giving the leaders of all the major countries access to buttons that can launch missiles and vaporize unsuspecting citizens. I think a better system would be if every world leader had to walk around with a sack of explosives on his back and every citizen had access to a wristwatch button that would detonate it. My concept has many benefits beyond the obvious entertainment factor and the reduced risk of being vaporized by an incoming missile. For one thing, there would no longer be any such thing as a "slow news day." And the boring pack of lies called the State of the Union speech would last about thirty seconds. I have to think taxes would be abolished altogether. We wouldn't need all the tax money anyway: The military would be unnecessary and the economic stimulus from eliminating taxes would make all the poor people incredibly wealthy, or so I've been told. And if we needed a highway or a dam built, we could give our president a trowel and then place one finger menacingly over the wristwatch button and say, "Start working, Goober." I realize that my concept would degrade the prestige of the presidency, but I don't think that prestige was doing me any good anyway.

Speaking of world leaders, there's still time to join Dogbert's New Ruling Class (DNRC) and rule by his side when he conquers the planet and makes everyone else our domestic servants. To become a member of the DNRC, just sign up for the free *Dilbert* newsletter that is distributed whenever I feel like it, usually four times a year.

To subscribe or unsubscribe, go to www.dilbert.com. If you have problems with the automated subscription method, write to newsletter@unitedmedia.com.

S. Adams

Scott Adams

12

24

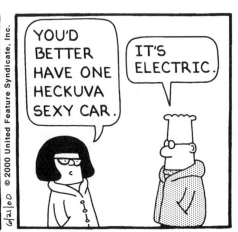

RATBERT THE CONCIERGE

I'D LIKE A DATE WITH A WOMAN WHO THINKS I'M HOT.

REMEMBER, YOU PROMISED YOU WOULD DO ANY ERRAND FOR EMPLOYEES.

TELL ME AGAIN HOW HOT I AM.

COMPANY CONCIERGE

I DON'T HAVE TIME FOR MY DOCTOR APPOINTMENT.

GO IN MY PLACE AND TELL HIM YOU'RE HAVING TROUBLE SLEEPING AT YOUR DESK.

AND DON'T LET HIM SWEET-TALK YOU ABOUT DIET AND EXERCISE. I WANT PILLS!

COMPANY CONCIERGE

I NEED AN ALIBI.

THE POLICE WILL TRY TO BEAT THE TRUTH OUT OF YOU, BUT DON'T LET THEM BREAK YOU!

I ALSO NEED LYE... AND A BARREL...

BETTER YET, MAKE THAT TWO BARRELS.

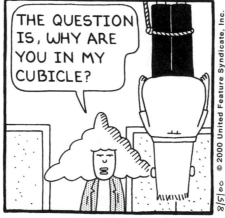

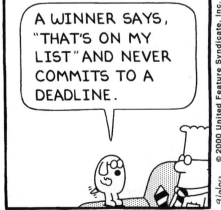

65

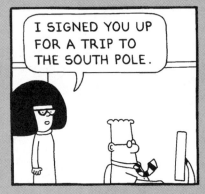

WE HAVE A GIGANTIC DATABASE FULL OF CUSTOMER BEHAVIOR INFORMATION.

EXCELLENT. WE CAN USE NON-LINEAR MATH AND DATA MINING TECHNOLOGY TO OPTIMIZE OUR RETAIL CHANNELS!

IF THAT'S THE SAME THING AS SPAM, WE'RE HAVING A GOOD MEETING HERE.

CATBERT: EVIL H.R. DIRECTOR

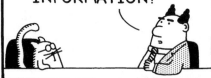

WHAT'S THE MOST EVIL WAY TO USE OUR DATABASE OF CUSTOMER INFORMATION?

SHOULD WE SELL OUR MAILING LISTS, SPAM WITHOUT MERCY, OR JUST BLACK-MAIL CUSTOMERS?

UM... DO YOU HAVE ME IN THAT DATA-BASE?

WE KNOW ALL ABOUT YOUR CLUMPING PROBLEMS.

THE DOGBERT TEMP AGENCY USES GENETIC ENGINEERING TO GROW OUR OWN WORKERS.

ISN'T THAT DANGEROUS?

I WEAR SAFETY GOGGLES.

I'M THE NEW TEMP.

UM... I'M ALICE.

93

WALLY, WE CAN'T FIND OUR CPR DUMMY. I NEED YOUR HELP.

FINDING IT?

YES, ASSUMING YOU CAN DO THAT WHILE LYING ON YOUR BACK WITH YOUR MOUTH OPEN.

THE COMPANY WILL BE HOLDING MANDATORY CPR TRAINING FOR ALL EMPLOYEES.

GAA!!

I AM SURROUNDED BY PEAR-SHAPED, BEEF-EATING, MIDDLE-AGED MEN WHO I PREFER NOT TO TOUCH.

UH-OH... I HOPE THAT'S JUST STRESS.

ASOK IS DOWN. DOES ANYONE KNOW CPR?

IS CPR THE ONE WHERE WE TAKE HIS KIDNEY AND LEAVE HIM IN A TUB OF ICE?

UM... I DON'T THINK SO.

WE'D BETTER STRIP HIM AND SHAVE HIM JUST IN CASE.

OKAY, WE HAVE ONE VOTE FOR USING CPR, ONE VOTE FOR THE HEIMLICH MANEUVER...

AND TWO VOTES FOR SNEAKING UP BEHIND HIM AND YELLING "BOO."

I DON'T SEE HOW WE CAN GET BEHIND HIM.

WHAT IF WE DRILL A HOLE FROM BELOW?

I'LL SEE IF THE GUYS IN MARKETING KNOW FIRST AID.

REALLY? I PICKED THAT INTERN IN OUR ENGINEERING DEAD POOL!

APPARENTLY OUR TEAM-BUILDING POTLUCK LUNCH DIDN'T TAKE.

I'M ALIVE!

WHICH ONE OF YOU ANGELS ADMINISTERED THE LIFE-SAVING CPR?

SPEAKING OF "LIFESAVERS," I COULD SURE USE ONE RIGHT NOW.

WE DON'T HAVE ENOUGH ENGINEERS TO HANDLE ALL THE REQUESTS FOR SALES SUPPORT.

BUILD AN ONLINE DATABASE TO LOG ALL THE REQUESTS.

IT MIGHT LOOK AS IF I'M STARING AT YOU WITH A MIXTURE OF CONTEMPT AND DIS-BELIEF, BUT I'M ACTUALLY MEDITATING.

IS THAT WHAT YOU WANTED?

I'M NOT SAYING.

IF I TELL YOU IT'S GOOD, YOU'LL RUB IT IN MY FACE AT YOUR PERFORMANCE REVIEW.

I'M SORRY.

SEE HOW YOU ARE?

DOGBERT CONSULTS

I'VE BEEN TOLD TO MAKE A SUCCESSION PLAN.

THE PLAN SHOULD SAY WHAT TO DO IF I DIE.

I CAN HELP.

AND IF SATAN MAKES YOU STAND IN FLAMING WORMS UP TO YOUR NOSE, TRY STANDING ON YOUR TIPTOES FOR ETERNITY.

I WORRY THAT CASUAL DRESS DAYS ENCOURAGE FLIRTATIOUS BEHAVIOR.

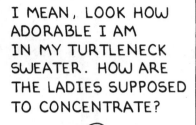

I MEAN, LOOK HOW ADORABLE I AM IN MY TURTLENECK SWEATER. HOW ARE THE LADIES SUPPOSED TO CONCENTRATE?

DO YOU THINK I SHOULD PUT WARNING CONES AROUND MY CUBICLE?

CASUAL DRESS DAY IS HURTING OUR PRODUCTIVITY. WE NEED TO CANCEL IT.

IS IT POSSIBLE THAT OUR REAL PROBLEMS ARE CAUSED BY IRRATIONAL MANAGEMENT?

NO, I THINK COMFORTABLE PANTS ARE THE PROBLEM.

SOUNDS RIGHT.

THERE WILL BE NO MORE CASUAL DRESS DAYS.

WE BELIEVE THAT EMPLOYEES WORK HARDER WHEN THEY ARE WEARING UNCOMFORTABLE CLOTHES.

I FEEL ALL MOTIVATED BUT I CAN'T LIFT MY ARMS.

THE AD AGENCY

IS IT WISE TO INSULT ALL OF THESE MINORITY GROUPS IN OUR COMMERCIAL?

WHAT'S THE WORST THING THAT COULD HAPPEN?

DOES OUR COMPANY HAVE TO SPIT ON A FLAG?

THAT'S IT; YOU'RE ON MY "DIFFICULT CLIENT" LIST NOW.

THE "EXACTLY" MAN

YOUR IDEA WON'T WORK. NO ONE WOULD BUY THIS KIND OF PRODUCT.

WE ALREADY SELL TEN MILLION OF THESE PER YEAR. MY IDEA JUST MAKES THEM BETTER.

EXACTLY!!

?

THE "EXACTLY" MAN

EVERYTHING YOU SAID IN THE MEETING WAS WRONG. HERE'S THE PROOF.

EXACTLY!!

OKAY, I'M NOT EVEN SURE THAT WAS A HUMANOID RESPONSE.

DISCOUNT BROKERAGE

I NEED AN ESTATE PLAN FOR AFTER I PASS AWAY.

HERE'S A PLAN: STAY DEAD. NO ONE LIKES A ZOMBIE.

WHAT ABOUT GIFTS?

ZOMBIES MAKE BAD GIFTS.

DISCOUNT BROKERAGE

WHEN YOU OPEN AN ACCOUNT, YOU'LL GET A FREE DART BOARD AND A MONKEY.

IF YOUR BALANCE DROPS BELOW FIVE HUNDRED DOLLARS, WE'LL ORDER THE MONKEY TO KILL YOU.

WELL, THINK ABOUT IT AND GET BACK TO ME.

DISCOUNT BROKERAGE

CAN YOU GIVE ME FREE INVESTMENT ADVICE?

SURE

GIVE ME ALL OF YOUR MONEY NOW NOW NOW!!

WHAT IF I PAID FOR SOME ADVICE?

IT'S THE SAME EXCEPT MY EARS DON'T FLIP UP IN A THREATENING MANNER.

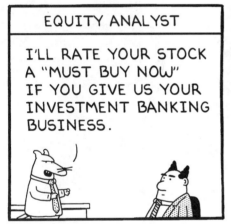

THIS IS THE ELBONIAN FULFILLMENT SERVICE. HOW MAY I THWART YOU?

GRUNT GRUNT GRUNT GRUNT GRUNT

OKAY, IT WASN'T FUNNY THE FIRST 300 TIMES EITHER.

THE RESULTS OF OUR CUSTOMER SATISFACTION SURVEY ARE IN.

83% SPAT AT THEIR TELEPHONES UNTIL THEY DIED OF DEHYDRATION.

WE'RE CALLING THAT GROUP "THE LUCKY ONES."

HELLO, IS THIS THE SALES DEPARTMENT?

MAY YOU DIE A THOUSAND DEATHS BY CHOKING ON YOUR OWN BILE!

A SUPERVISOR MAY BE MONITORING THIS CALL FOR QUALITY CONTROL.

IT'S GOOD.